AMERICA'S ARMED FORCES

The U.S. ARMY

M. K. BARBIER

WORLD ALMANAC® LIBRARY

Please visit our web site at: www.garethstevens.com
For a free color catalog describing our list of high-quality books,
call 1-800-542-2595 (USA) or 1-800-387-3178 (Canada).

Library of Congress Cataloging-in-Publication Data

Barbier, Mary.
    The U.S. Army / by Mary Barbier.
        p. cm. — (America's armed forces)
    Includes bibliographical references and index.
    ISBN-13: 978-0-8368-5680-4 (lib. bdg.)   ISBN-13: 978-0-8368-5687-3 (softcover)
    ISBN-10: 0-8368-5680-5 (lib. bdg.)   ISBN-10: 0-8368-5687-2 (softcover)
    1. United States. Army—Juvenile literature.   2. United States. Army—Vocational
guidance—Juvenile literature.   I. Title: United States Army.   II. Title.   III. Series.
    UA25.B23   2004
    355'.00973—dc22   2004042791

First published in 2005 by
World Almanac® Library
An imprint of Gareth Stevens Publishing
1 Reader's Digest Road
Pleasantville, NY 10570-7000 USA

Copyright © 2005 by World Almanac® Library.

Developed by Amber Books Ltd.
Editor: James Bennett
Designer: Colin Hawes
Photo research: Sandra Assersohn, Natasha Jones
World Almanac® Library editor: Mark Sachner
World Almanac® Library art direction: Tammy West
World Almanac® Library production: Jessica Morris

Picture Acknowledgements
TRH: cover, 4, 6, 8, 9 (both), 10, 12, 13, 14, 15, 16, 17, 20, 21, 24, 26, 27, 28, 32, 33, 34 (U.S. Army),
35 (US Army), 37 (US D.O.D.), 40; Corbis: 36; U.S. D.O.D: 5 (U.S. Army), 11 (U.S. Army), 29, 30,
38, 41, 43; Topham Picturepoint: 18, 19, 22, 23. Maps: Patrick Mulrey.

Printed in the United States

2 3 4 5 6 7 8 9 10 09 08 07

About the Author

M. K. BARBIER is a historian and writer who currently holds the position of Assistant
Professor at Mississippi State University. She was previously the John M. Olin
Postdoctoral Fellow in International Security Studies at Yale University. She earned
her Ph.D. at the University of Southern Mississippi. Her published books include
Kursk: The Greatest Tank Battle Ever Fought and *Strategy and Tactics: Infantry Warfare*.

Table of Contents

Introduction

Right: A soldier of the 173rd Airborne Brigade plots a fire mission in Vietnam in May 1965.

The United States Army has had a long and varied history. The Army has produced such leaders as George Washington, Ulysses S. Grant, Robert E. Lee, George S. Patton, and Colin Powell. The Army has served in every major engagement since the Revolutionary War and adjusted to social and political changes along the way.

There are many reasons why people enlist in the Army. For some, the Army provides the opportunity to receive a college education. For others, the Army is a career; and for many it fulfills a desire to protect the freedoms of the United States. Historically, many enlisted in the Army because they believed that it would offer them adventure. The horrors experienced by soldiers during World Wars I and II—and later during the wars in Korea and Vietnam—showed them that war was brutal, and when their service was over, most soldiers just wanted to return home. As the United States became a superpower, the Cold War (1945–1991) saw the United States upholding U.S.-style democracy around the world. During the Vietnam war (1959–1975)—a war that proved to be "unwinnable"—many Americans became critical of the U.S. government's policies abroad and, as the chief agent of those policies, the Army as well.

In recent years, the Army has had to address other controversies in addition to its military policies, including sexual harassment of female personnel and the treatment of homosexuals in the military. Both issues have caused the Army to reassess its policies, ensuring all people are treated fairly, without compromising its ability to function as one of the greatest military arms the world has ever seen.

Left: An officer inspects cadets at the United States Military Academy at West Point. Whether at attention or at rest, the cadets must always be professional and alert.

Right: One of the best known commanders of the Revolutionary Army, George Washington, in a painting by American artist Edward Hicks (1780–1849).

There was no army prior to the Revolutionary War (1775–1783). The British government, the sovereign ruler of the American colonies, sent forces to protect its interests if a situation arose that called for military action. However, the colonies were growing and developing, and as more people came to America, the British government was forced to spend a great deal of money protecting them. In 1764, the British government imposed taxes on imports to the colonies to eliminate debt and defray the costs of protecting them.

Many of the colonists objected to the new taxes and to the continued presence of the British soldiers in the colonies. Much to the colonists' dismay, the British soldiers had been assigned duties beyond protection. The soldiers were also enforcing the new taxation laws. Although many colonists disagreed with the burdensome taxes, they would have been happy if the taxes had been repealed. Severing ties with Britain was not on their minds. They were loyal subjects to their king. Many colonists favored **boycotting** the taxed goods. While this had some effect, the British government continued to impose taxes. Delegates from the 13 colonies met in Philadelphia in 1774 to discuss the matter. The meeting became known as the First Continental Congress. Although the Continental Congress did not necessarily want war, it urged the colonies to gather military supplies and prepare to defend colonial rights should independence from Britain become the only option.

The Revolution Begins

In April 1775, General George Gage, the British governor and military commander of Massachusetts, ordered his soldiers to close the Massachusetts

George Washington

The best-known colonial commander was George Washington (1732–1799). A Southern colonial aristocrat, Washington was a lieutenant colonel in the Virginia **militia** at the age of 22. His leadership qualities led to his appointment as colonel and commander-in-chief of the Virginia militia in 1755. Because of his military experience and his position, the Continental Congress unanimously chose Washington to command the newly formed Continental Army on June 15, 1775.

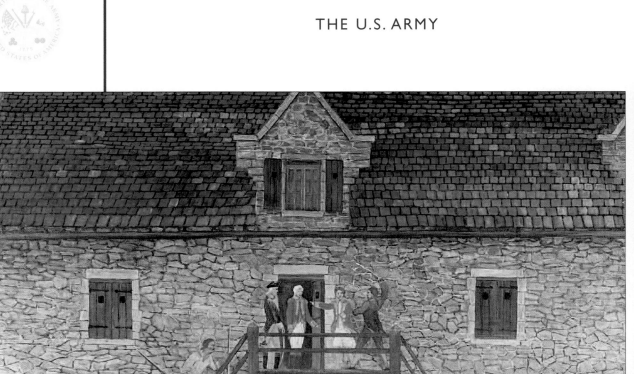

Above: American troops surprise the British garrison at Fort Ticonderoga.

Who Were the Militia?

Each colony raised its own militia force. The militiamen elected their officers, who were frequently from the upper classes. For a time, the untrained militiamen provided the backbone of the Continental Army.

assembly to prevent people from discussing rebellion. He also ordered his troops to confiscate weapons and ammunition. Colonial militiamen were prepared, having been warned of the British advance by a silversmith and patriot, Paul Revere (1735–1818). They fought British troops at Lexington and Concord, defeating the British resoundingly and sending them back to Boston. Two months later, the Continental Congress authorized a Continental Army and chose George Washington to lead it. Despite the fervor for independence, the new army faced a lack of weapons and money to purchase food, ammunition, and other supplies. In addition, many militiamen were farmers who returned home during planting and harvesting seasons, making manpower a constant problem. George Washington once complained that his force had been "reduced to a mere handful of men, indeed, reduced to a mere *nothing*."

A Rebellion in Earnest

The British army was trained in the European method of warfare. European armies used linear tactics: the opposing armies lined up facing each other, marched to within firing range, and then fired. The newly formed Continental Army, commanded by George Washington, was trained to fight in the same way as the British. Although the colonists did use some **guerilla** tactics, most **battles** of the American Revolution were fought like European battles.

After the Revolutionary War and the creation of the newly independent United States of America, the Continental Congress wanted to disband the Continental Army. A debate over the type and size of the nation's army began and continued into the next century. Americans did not want a large permanent army, fearing the same problems they experienced under the British military— namely that soldiers would dictate or enforce laws. This trepidation prompted Congress to reduce the professional force in 1784. Soon, problems in the new nation—battles on the frontier with Native Americans—and outside the new nation, especially skirmishes with Britain and Mexico, would force Congress to increase the army temporarily.

Above: On July 9, 1776, American colonists tore down the statue of King George III in New York City. William Walcutt painted this revolutionary scene on canvas in 1854.

Left: In July 1775, the Continental Congress considered the role of the militia in the difficult times ahead.

Right: The U.S. Army frequently clashed with Native Americans during the nineteenth century. This painting by Frederic Remington (1860–1909) portrays the aftermath of the Battle of Warbonnet Creek, Nebraska.

The Army of the nineteenth century faced military challenges on many fronts. One of the Army's most demanding and longstanding functions was to fight the U.S. government's campaigns against Native American peoples. The Army lacked the manpower, funding, and public support to create a well-trained, well-equipped force. Yet at the same time the government demanded that the Army enforce its policies of westward expansion against Native peoples who resisted this expansion.

Campaigns Against American Indians

Many of the fiercest battles between the Army and Native Americans were in the Great Plains, in the center of the North American continent. From 1855 until about 1877, the Sioux, Cheyenne, Comanche, Kiowa, and other tribes fought the Army in a series of actions. One notable encounter was the defeat of Lieutenant Colonel George Custer at the Battle of the Little Bighorn in southern Montana in 1876. More commonly known as Custer's Last Stand, this battle was between the Seventh United States Cavalry and the Sioux and Northern Cheyenne. The Black Hills in Dakota have always been sacred to the Sioux. When gold was discovered there, prospectors poured in. The Army was called in to suppress an Indian uprising. Custer attacked a large Indian village in the valley of the Little Bighorn river with two companies of the Seventh Cavalry. Custer and all of the 225 men under his command that day were massacred by an overwhelming force of between 2,000 and 4,000 Indians.

Another famous battle occurred at Wounded Knee in today's South Dakota. This battle arose over the rights of the Sioux people to participate in their Ghost Dance ritual. A Piaute prophet named Wovoka taught the Ghost Dance to the Sioux with the promise that, if they wore special shirts while dancing, it would make the warriors invulnerable to soldiers' bullets, cause the

West Point

In March 1802, bowing to pressure from President Thomas Jefferson, Congress passed an act creating the United States Military Academy at West Point. Jefferson wanted an officer-training institution to provide the Army with intellectual direction and doctrine. Originally, the academy was an artillery and engineering institution. The curriculum at West Point has since expanded to include military, social and natural sciences, and the humanities.

Right: Many Sioux men, women, and children were killed by the Seventh Cavalry at Wounded Knee, South Dakota, in 1890. This photograph shows the unpleasant task of gathering the dead after the battle.

disappearance of white men from their lands, and bring a period of peace and prosperity to Indian people. Many followers of Wovoka practiced the Ghost Dance, and the government, playing on fears that the ceremonial gathering of the Sioux would lead to attacks against whites, used the ceremony as an excuse to act against the Indians. In December 1890 the U.S. Army arrested the Sioux leader Sitting Bull. As he was being led away, over the objections of his supporters, a gunfight erupted. Thirteen people, including Sitting Bull, were killed. His followers fled, and the Seventh Cavalry pursued the Sioux to Wounded Knee Creek. On December 29, 1890, someone fired a gun and the army began shooting. Estimates place the number of Indians killed between 150 and 370 Sioux men, women, and children, most of whom were unarmed.

Such battles led the U.S. government to impose a policy whereby Native people were forcibly removed from their lands and placed onto reservations. The Army was called upon to carry out the enforced relocation. The Indian Removal Act of 1830, implemented by President Andrew Jackson, resulted in uprooting entire tribes from their homelands and their forced resettlement beyond the Mississippi. One of the most dramatic and tragic migrations was the forced removal of the Cherokee nation. Between 1838 and 1839, thousands of Cherokees were forced by the Army to march from their homeland in the southeastern United States to

Indian Territory (present-day Oklahoma). Along the way, about 4,000 Cherokee and members of other southeastern Native groups died from starvation, disease, and exposure or in stockades while awaiting removal. Because of the extreme hardships and many deaths suffered on this journey, the path was called The Trail of Tears. By the 1890s the American frontier was gone, and most Native American resistance had been quelled.

The War of 1812

The War of 1812 had its origins in the British practice of impressment, the seizure of U.S. seamen for service in the British navy. The British claimed they were seizing British citizens avoiding military duty by "hiding out" on U.S. ships. The truth was that both British and U.S. citizens were seized. Public outrage over impressments reached its height after an incident between the U.S. naval frigate *Chesapeake* and a British vessel, the *Leopard*. In June 1807, the *Leopard* approached the *Chesapeake* off the eastern U.S. coast and demanded to

Above: In March 1886, General George Crook met with Apache chief Geronimo, who is sitting, facing the camera. Crook is the man sitting second from the right.

search the ship for British deserters. Commander James Barron, of the *Chesapeake*, refused and the *Leopard* opened fire. A number of U.S. sailors were killed or wounded, and the *Chesapeake* was forced to surrender. President James Madison requested a declaration of war to protect U.S. ships and stop the British impressments. It was granted, but the Army was not ready for war. The British army had 300,000 men, while the U.S. army had 11,000. The government called up 450,000 short-term militiamen. The problem with relying upon militiamen was the question of whether they were allowed to serve outside of the country; some refused to leave U.S. territory. In addition, the militiamen had little or no training. Consequently, the Army did not perform well initially.

The Army planned three offensives against the British in Canada in 1812, but they failed. In 1814, British forces faced little opposition as they attacked the east coast, briefly capturing Washington, D.C. and burning the Capitol and the White House. The Army's most noted victory of the war, the Battle of New Orleans, was fought on January 8, 1815. The battle should not have taken place. Britain and the United States had signed a peace agreement at a meeting in Europe, but news of this had not yet reached the U.S. or British forces. After the war, the Army again had to fight for its existence. Despite support for a larger army, Congress reduced the Army to 8,200 men in 1817. By 1823, only 6,000 men remained.

The Mexican War

Later in the nineteenth century, tensions between the United States and Mexico increased over territory that once belonged to Mexico and is now part of the U.S. West and Southwest. In 1836, Texans rebelled against Mexican rule and declared independence as a republic. In 1845, Texas requested admission to the United States. Admission was granted, but Mexico disapproved of Texas becoming part of the United States. Hostilities erupted in 1846 when U.S. troops occupied territory at the mouth of the Rio Grande and were attacked by Mexican forces. Although not adequately prepared for war, experience and better weapons helped the U.S. Army. As in the past, manpower shortages were a constant challenge; both volunteers and the **regular army** were important in the Mexican War.

Below: The United States and Mexico were at war from 1846 until 1848. Hostilities ended after American forces captured Mexico City.

In the Battle of Buena Vista in 1847, Zachary Taylor led his troops to the first great U.S. victory of the Mexican War (1846–1848). Buena Vista was a village in the state of Coahuila, Mexico. A series of U.S. victories, including the capture of Mexico City, resulted in the end of hostilities by 1848 and a subsequent increase in the Southwestern area of the United States.

The Mexican War marked a change in the nature of the Army. The role of local and state militias declined, and more emphasis was placed on a regular army supplemented by volunteers. Many of the officers who led troops for the first time in Mexico brought that experience to the next major conflict—the Civil War (1861–1865) which would have an even greater impact than previous conflicts and continues to resonate in the consciousness of Americans today.

The Civil War

Between 1848 and 1861, heated debates over the expansion of slavery split the nation. Since the federal government at this time did not have authority over the practice or abolition of slavery, the states had to work it out among themselves. In 1820, The Missouri Compromise was implemented as a hopeful solution to

Right: One of the Union generals who led the North to victory in the Civil War was General Ulysses S. Grant (center, wearing a hat), pictured here with his staff.

the divisive issue of slavery. In this agreement, Missouri was admitted to the Union as a slave state and Maine was admitted as a free state to keep the balance between slave and free states in the Senate. In addition, slavery was excluded from the Louisiana Territory. A line was drawn from Missouri's southern boundary, and slavery was not allowed in the territory north of it, with the exception of Missouri.

Tensions between free states and slave states increased as the country grew and the struggle over the issue of slavery continued. Another short-term fix was the Compromise Measure of 1850. The measure admitted California as a free state and set up territorial governments in the remainder of the territory won from Mexico. This compromise was also temporary, however, and the gap widened between slave states and free states. South Carolina was the first Southern state to **secede**, followed by 10 more slavery-supporting states. They called themselves the Confederate States of America. As the nation divided, so did the Army. Many West Point officers, such as Robert E. Lee, returned to the South, assuming leadership positions in the Confederate Army. Other officers, such as Ulysses

Below: The most famous Confederate commander was General Robert E. Lee (wearing an open coat), seen here with his staff.

Robert E. Lee

Robert E. Lee, generally considered one of the nation's best tacticians, graduated second in his 1829 West Point class. Between then and 1846, he received various assignments in military engineering. He participated in many battles during the Mexican War, including the battle for Mexico City. When the Civil War broke out, Lee refused field command of the Union Army and returned to Virginia to serve in the Confederate Army. He achieved many remarkable victories over his Union opponents before suffering his worst defeat at Gettysburg.

Right: In the summer of 1863, Lee took his forces north into Pennsylvania. An accidental meeting with Union forces resulted in three days of heavy fighting at Gettysburg. Following this defeat, Lee would never again venture north.

S. Grant, remained in the Union Army. Although many men flocked to both armies, neither side was really ready for war.

The North's three-part strategy included capturing Richmond, Virginia (the capital of the Confederacy); seizing the Mississippi River; and setting up a naval blockade of the South. The Confederacy had an effective navy, which included a number of "blockade runners", which slipped through the Northern ships trying to stop goods reaching the South. The South was, however, short of **munitions** factories and other industries to supply the war. In addition, because the population of the South was lower than that of the North, it suffered a shortage of manpower.

During the war, both the Union and Confederate armies used similar weapons. Both sides used rifle muskets and some rifled artillery. The **infantry** attacked in long lines of soldiers two ranks deep, and casualties were high because the Civil War saw the largest armies ever to have fought in America. In 1864, during one month of fighting, 55,000 of 115,000 Union soldiers died. Confederate casualties were equally high. Because of its larger population, the North could replenish its army more easily than the South and added many Irish immigrants to its ranks who were eager to fight for the North. Realizing this, General Grant launched several battles to inflict large numbers of casualties. Because his forces were unable to recover from their mounting losses, General Lee ended the four-year war, surrendering on April 12, 1865, at Appomattox Court House, Virginia.

Weapon Developments

The North and South continued to use smooth-bore weapons during the war, but most muskets and some cannon were rifled. They had grooves on the inside of their barrels which gave musket balls a spin when they were fired, making them more accurate.

Ulysses S. Grant

The famous Ulysses S. Grant entered West Point in 1839. Later, unhappy with his Army assignments, Grant resigned, but with the outbreak of the Civil War, he returned as a colonel in the 21st Illinois Infantry. He was promoted to brigadier general two months later. Grant impressed President Abraham Lincoln with his intelligence and military tactics. Grant soon became general-in-chief of the Union Army. Grant's forces inflicted heavy casualties on Lee's soldiers, pushing them south from an area known as The Wilderness, in northeast Virginia, to Petersburg, Virginia.

Chapter 3
The Early Twentieth-Century Army

The battle of Malate, Philippines
night of July 31st 1898

Right: During the Spanish-American War in 1898, U.S. infantrymen took on Spanish troops in the Phillippines in skirmishes such as the Battle of Malate, illustrated here.

Although the Army's size declined in the years following the Civil War, its responsibilities did not. Beyond protecting the country from external threats, the Army occupied the defeated South during the period known as Reconstruction, participated in the forced removal of Native Americans onto reservations, and was even called into action against U.S. citizens. In the late 1870s, for example, when workers organized strikes to protest against working conditions, the Army was sent to subdue the strikers and their supporters.

The Army often had insufficient men and supplies to carry out its duties. In the late nineteenth century, its involvement outside the United States would increase. As trade grew between the United States and Latin American countries, U.S. activists became concerned about the living conditions people endured in these countries. When a revolution began in Cuba in 1898, many Americans supported Cubans who wanted independence from Spain, and when the USS *Maine* blew up in the harbor in the Cuban capital, Havana, Spain was blamed for the incident. Congress declared war against Spain to guarantee Cuba's independence. During the Spanish-American War of 1898, the U.S. military fought Spanish forces in Cuba and the Philippines. Because the Army had insufficient equipment and weapons, many soldiers, especially volunteers, trained without weapons and had none until they went to Cuba. Despite these deficiencies, the United States was victorious.

In the early years of the twentieth century, a major problem faced by the Army was the age of its weapons. The Army replaced its old rifles and revolvers with new weapons that were more efficient and powerful. The Army also adopted new

Below: African American soldiers such as these in the 369th Infantry Regiment of the 93rd Division served with distinction during World War I. The Buffalo Soldier tradition survived through World War II, after which the U.S. Army was no longer segregated.

Buffalo Soldiers

On July 23, 1866, in recognition of the 180,000 African American soldiers who served in the Union Army, Congress ordered that one-fifth of the cavalry and one-eleventh of the infantry would consist of African American enlisted men. All officers were white. The African American soldiers serving on the frontier in cavalry units were known as Buffalo Soldiers.

field guns, or artillery. These weapons were very accurate and deadly, far more than the artillery used during the nineteenth century. The Army changed in other ways, too. There was a reorganization of its high command, and the Army invested in a new invention: aircraft. The Army now needed to fund building planes and training pilots to fly them, so it did not have the money for developing the technology some European armies had, such as tanks and submarines.

World War I

In 1914, World War I broke out between the Central Powers—Germany, Austria-Hungary, and Turkey—and the Allies, which included Great Britain, France, and Russia. The United States was determined to stay neutral despite the sinking of the unarmed RMS *Lusitania*, a British liner carrying U.S. tourists, by a German U-boat in 1915. Despite this resolve the country joined the war in 1917 after Germany resumed its policy of unrestricted submarine warfare. Many officers believed that World War I, then called the Great War, would be a war of maneuver and that cavalry would play a major role. They soon learned that this would not be the case. In Europe, both sides dug trenches stretching more than

Right: World War I was characterized by trench warfare. These U.S. soldiers served in the trenches near Ancerville, France, in March 1918.

375 miles (600 km) through Belgium, France, and Switzerland. Battles lasted several months and were devastating in terms of casualties. For example, the Battle of the Somme, July 1–November 9, 1916, saw more than one million British, French, and German casualties. Despite horrific conditions in the trenches, U.S. forces in France made major contributions leading to eventual victory.

The United States had been preparing for three years before entering World War I. In 1916, Congress approved an increase in the size of the Army. The president also called up 400,000 National Guardsmen—a reserve force of volunteer soldiers. Congress also created a reserve force of officers and enlisted men. Congress passed the Selective Service Act of May 1917, authorizing a draft of men between 21 and 30 and an increase in the National Guard. Approximately 200,000 African Americans served overseas in **segregated** units under white officers. Most black soldiers, however, were relegated to labor and supply units. Men were not the only citizens prepared to serve. Many women volunteered. While some nurses had overseas duty, most did not receive military rank. In addition, they received little or no pay.

Above: In 1919, John "Black Jack" Pershing, General of the Armies of the United States, participated in a parade in London that celebrated the end of World War I.

The Army After World War I

World War I saw the largest U.S. military mobilization up to that time, and brought about shifts in industrial production to support the millions of soldiers. Another big change would occur during World War II, when women entered the workforce to fill in for men serving overseas. For the first time, military successes were linked with industry, agriculture, and other sectors of the economy. Although a minimal occupation force remained in Germany until 1923, most soldiers returned home after the Allied victory. By the end of 1919, Congress had reduced the size of the Army yet again, from one million to 137,000. Despite limited manpower and money, the Army continued to improve. While it initially neglected the tank, then in its experimental phase, it did invest in rifle, artillery, and other weapons development. Officers, such as General George C. Marshall, pushed for participation in war games: training exercises in simulated battles.

Chapter 4
World War II (1939–1945)

Right: Disembarking from a landing craft, American troops storm the beaches of Normandy, France, during the Allied invasion on June 6, 1944—D-Day.

In 1938, Germany took control of Austria and part of Czechoslovakia. In 1939, Germany took over the rest of Czechoslovakia and invaded Poland. Britain and France declared war on Germany, and fighting in Europe began. Although the United States declared its neutrality, President Franklin D. Roosevelt ordered an increase in the Army and the National Guard. Congress approved the money necessary to prepare for a potential war, and in the summer of 1939, the Army staged war games to identify strengths and weaknesses. According to General Marshall, the Army Chief of Staff, the Army was "relatively less prepared today than it was in 1917." Marshall meant that after World War I, the government substantially reduced the size and funding of the armed forces.

Although many resisted the modernization and expansion of the military, growing Japanese and German aggression in the mid-1930s persuaded Congress to authorize an increase in the Army. With the outbreak of war in Europe, there was an increase in the production of wartime materials. By September 1940, Congress passed the Burke-Wadsworth Act, which authorized the first ever peacetime draft in United States history. Increasing the size of the military did not, however, mean that the Army would be as prepared as it should be if the United States were to become involved in the conflict in Europe.

Marshall was determined to remedy this and scheduled training exercises for two years. His goal was to engage the United States in combined arms operations, as the Germans did when they quickly defeated Poland, Norway, Belgium, and France. The Germans used *Blitzkrieg* tactics, relying on aircraft, tanks, and infantry working together. The aircraft disrupted Allied troop movements and organization. Then, tanks broke through front lines, drove to the rear, and surrounded Allied troops. Finally, the infantry held the captured territory.

The United States Enters the War

On December 7, 1941, Japanese planes attacked Pearl Harbor in Hawaii. On December 8, the United States declared war on Japan. Three days later, Germany and Italy declared war on the United States. Men flocked

George C. Marshall

A proponent of war games, General Marshall learned from his experiences in World War I. After arriving in France in 1917, two factors showed the seriousness of the situation: the number of French women in mourning and the poor state of U.S. troops serving there. Consequently, Marshall became determined to better train and exercise his troops.

The Louisiana Maneuvers

The 1940 Louisiana Maneuvers were the first large-scale war games in the United States. Involving 70,000 soldiers and costing $28 million, the two-week maneuvers allowed troops to test tactics similar to the German *blitzkrieg*. As a result, Congress allocated additional funds for exercises, and when troops went overseas for World War II, they were better prepared than soldiers in 1917.

Above: Carrying only a single machine gun, the M2A1 Tank was used by the U.S. Army for training purposes in the years before World War II but did not see combat.

to join the Army. This influx and the subsequent need for weapons, equipment, and training were immediate concerns. The government called on factories to provide the equipment needed to win the war, ordering aircraft, tanks, artillery, flamethrowers, guns, ammunition, uniforms, and food. Of course, women also wanted to contribute. Many worked in industry, taking over jobs that men who were away fighting had done. Other women joined the military. Unlike during World War I, women received rank and pay. Most served as nurses, clerical personnel, and drivers. Some worked as journalists and pilots.

The European Theater

World War II was a far-reaching conflict between the **Allies** (or Allied Forces), which included the U.S., Britain, Canada, France, and the Soviet Union, and the **Axis** (or Axis Powers), comprising Italy, Germany, and Japan.

In November 1942, U.S. and British soldiers, in their first joint amphibious operation, landed in North Africa, where the British had been fighting German and Italian troops. The landing went well, but the U.S. soldiers had trouble stopping German forces during the battle. American and British troops joined together to halt the Germans in the Battle of Kasserine Pass. Fighting in North Africa continued until May 1943 and ended in an Allied victory.

Having already achieved military success in the Mediterranean, the Allies decided to attack the Italian island of Sicily and then Italy proper. The night before Allied soldiers landed on Sicily on July 10, 1943, troops parachuted behind enemy lines. While the Italian soldiers put up little resistance, the German forces

fought hard until mid-August. In early September 1943, Allied forces landed in southern Italy, where the fighting was much more difficult. The Italians soon surrendered, but the Germans struggled fiercely for Italy. Rome fell to the Allies on June 4, 1944, yet the battle for Italy was not over.

In the meantime, the Allies were preparing for the largest amphibious invasion to date — the Battle of Normandy. After months of bombing by Allied planes, U.S., British, and Canadian troops landed on the Normandy

Above: Allied troops participating in Operation Torch land on the North African coast in 1942.

African Americans in the U.S. Army During World War II

More than 700,000 African American men volunteered to serve during World War II. Although 500,000 of them went overseas, most served in supply and construction units. Some African Americans did see combat, but in segregated units commanded by white officers. Some African Americans trained to be pilots in the Army Air Corps Program at Tuskegee, Alabama. These Tuskegee Airmen saw combat, primarily in Italy, where they also served in segregated units.

Below: African American P-51 Mustang pilots, based in Italy, prepare to escort bombers on a mission over Germany.

George S. Patton

One of the most noted U.S. generals was George S. Patton. He was brilliant, flamboyant, and controversial. A graduate of West Point, he served in France during World War I. While there, Patton joined the Army's tank corps and received command of the 304th Brigade. After the war, Patton rejoined the cavalry because the Army's armored weaponry was minimal. By 1941, Patton commanded the 2nd Armored Division and distinguished himself in Sicily. Although he did not participate in the invasion of France in 1944, Patton returned there in August 1944, commanding the Third Army. Patton shaped the development of U.S. tank warfare during World War II.

Left: After successful Allied amphibious landings on Sicily's north coast, Lieutenant Colonel Lyle Bernard (right) discusses strategy with General George S. Patton.

beaches on June 6, 1944, known as D-Day. Although the British and Canadians met resistance, Americans landing on Omaha Beach suffered the greatest losses—3,000 casualties on the first day alone. The Allies needed to stay in France, but it would not be easy. The fight across France and into

Above: U.S. troops in the Pacific Theater frequently found themselves fighting the enemy on jungle islands such as Guadalcanal, pictured here.

Germany was difficult. The Western Allies pushed the Germans east, and the Soviets pushed them west. On May 8, 1945, the war in Europe officially ended, but that did not mean war was over. The Allies continued to fight the Japanese in the Pacific Theater.

The Pacific Theater

The fighting in the Pacific was different from that in North Africa or Europe. There were more naval battles, especially between U.S. and Japanese aircraft carriers. In addition, the Japanese had captured many islands, and the Allies had to recapture them. U.S. Marines made amphibious landings, and after securing the beaches, Army infantrymen joined the battle. Fierce fighting occurred on islands such as Guadalcanal (August 1942–February 1943) and

Iwo Jima (February–March 1945), and both sides suffered heavy casualties. The Americans had one advantage: they were transmitting messages in an almost unbreakable code, based on the Navajo (Dineh) language. Frequently working under hazardous conditions, Navajo "code talkers" attached to both Army and Marine Corps units transmitted orders and reports in their own language, sending secure messages that were unintelligible to others, including the Japanese.

In August 1945, after the United States captured Iwo Jima and Okinawa, a U.S. invasion of Japan seemed the next step. Convinced that such an invasion would inflict huge U.S. losses with no guarantee of ending the war, President Harry S. Truman made a difficult and momentous decision—to drop two atomic bombs on the cities of Hiroshima and Nagasaki. Over 250,000 Japanese citizens died, causing Japan to surrender on August 14, 1945. While some U.S. soldiers remained in Germany and Japan as occupation forces, most returned home. They, like most Americans, believed that they had achieved peace, but it would not last. Just a few years later, the Army would once again find itself committed to battles overseas.

Native Americans in World War II

In 1924 the Snyder Act gave citizenship to Native Americans, making them eligible for the draft in World War II. However, conscription alone does not account for the disproportionate number of Native Americans who joined the armed services. More than 44,000 men and women, out of a total Native American population of fewer than 350,000, served with distinction between 1941 and 1945 in both European and Pacific theaters of war.

As well as serving in every branch of the armed forces, most notably as code talkers in the Pacific island campaigns, Native American men and women on the home front also participated in the war effort. More than 40,000 Indian people left their reservations to work in ordnance depots, factories, and other war industries. Native Americans also invested more than $50 million in war bonds and contributed generously to the Red Cross and the Army and Navy Relief societies.

Right: During the fighting in Vietnam, Army pilots helicoptered soldiers to various "hot spots" around the country. Here a CH-47 Chinook deposits 3rd Brigade troops into a secured landing zone on a mountain ridge.

Events before, during, and after World War II created distrust between the United States and the Soviet Union. This period was called the Cold War (1945–1991) because relations between the two countries were so tense at times that they were often on the brink of war, although actual fighting never took place. As a democracy, the United States is a nation whose government is ruled by its citizens, primarily through elected representatives. As a communist nation, the Soviet Union was run by a government that controlled everything, disbursing goods based on need. The two nations had differing philosophies and could not determine a way to resolve them. The result of these philosophical, political, and economic differences was a struggle between the two world powers for international dominance. While the two nations never militarily engaged each other directly, the Cold War was marked by several overseas conflicts pitting Western forces backed or represented by the United States against communist bloc nations led by the Soviet Union. The first of these conflicts was the Korean War, which began in 1950. The U.S. soldiers sent to Korea as part of a United Nations (U.N.) operation were part of an army in transition.

Left: In July 1950, soldiers of the 25th Infantry Division move up to the firing line in Korea. Because of President Truman's orders to desegregate the military, more African American troops found themselves assigned to combat units.

Douglas MacArthur

One of the most celebrated U.S. military commanders of the twentieth century was Douglas MacArthur. He graduated with honors from West Point in 1903. During the next 10 years, MacArthur served in the Philippines, Panama, and stateside, where he received an appointment to the War Department General Staff. During World War II, although his defense of the Philippines failed, MacArthur fulfilled his promise to return. In September 1945, he received the Japanese surrender aboard the USS Missouri. His greatest military success was during the Korean War with a landing at Inchon on September 15, 1950. In the spring of 1951, President Truman ordered MacArthur back to the United States for insubordination because MacArthur publicly advocated attacking China.

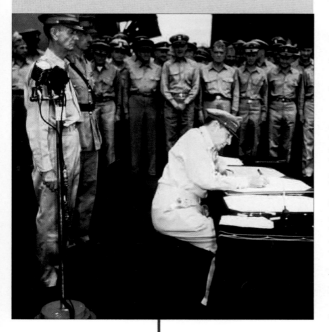

After World War II, four million troops had returned home, but another four million remained overseas as occupational forces. Due to increasing public pressure, the Army hurried the process by which it discharged men. Furthermore, national budget problems encouraged President Harry S Truman to agree to cuts in the armed forces. By 1947, although it required a minimum of four million men, the Army contained fewer than one million. When the Korean War (1950–1953) broke out, only 591,000 people remained in the Army. President Truman separated the Air Force (formerly the Army Air Corps) from the Army and made a new Uniform Code of Military Justice. In addition, Truman ordered the racial integration of the military. The Navy and the Air Force had to desegregate by June 1950. The Army had until 1954 to become fully integrated. With these revolutionary changes, the Army, like the other military branches, underwent reorganization and reduction. Consequently, it was not totally prepared when North Korea initiated hostilities.

The Korean War

The U.N. Security Council condemned the invasion of South Korea by communist North Korea in June 1950, and President Truman ordered General Douglas MacArthur to use U.S. troops in Japan to stop the North Koreans. Once again, the Army's size limited its abilities. During the first months of the war, U.S. and U.N. troops failed to stop the North Koreans. Furthermore, President Truman did not consider the Korean situation a major conflict. Consequently, the Army's access to resources was limited. The Soviet Union, he felt, was the major focus. Following his election as president in 1952, Dwight D. Eisenhower threatened to use every weapon available to end the stalemate if the North Koreans did not return to the negotiating table. Talks resumed, and the two sides signed an **armistice** in July 1953 to end the fighting.

The Korean War marked the U.S. military's increased role in world affairs. U.S. forces remained stationed around the world to meet the perceived threat of the Soviet Union. To be ready, the Army needed sufficient numbers of trained personnel ready to go overseas at a moment's notice.

Below: A six-man gun crew loads a 105mm howitzer preparing for a fire mission to support infantry troops northwest of Tuy Hoa, Vietnam, in 1968.

Above: Helicopters support U.S. 173rd Airborne troops during an assault in Vietnam.

The Vietnam War

During the 1950s, several officers traveled to South Vietnam to advise the Army of the Republic of Vietnam (ARVN). Over the next decade, advisor numbers increased from a handful of officers and enlisted men in 1950 to 17,000 by late 1963, when their role changed. They and the Green Berets, who were trained in guerrilla warfare, began going into the field with the ARVN. The U.S. military's commitment changed again in 1965 when troops went into battle. This escalation persuaded the government to reinstitute the draft, altering the nature of the forces in Vietnam. Originally, U.S. forces consisted of career soldiers. With the draft, **conscripts** joined them. Because enlistment terms were limited, there was a constant turnover, and units failed to develop cohesion. The U.S. Army also faced problems not previously encountered in other wars. Partly because of the availability of alcohol and drugs, some soldiers developed substance addictions, particularly to heroin, which was available in great abundance in Vietnam. Furthermore, the war required unconventional tactics since there were no clear front lines, creating new demands on soldiers' skills as military fighters and putting an even greater strain on their nerves.

The Vietnam War had several short- and long-term consequences for the Army. Because of the much publicized antiwar movement back home and the radically different nature of this war, some soldiers became disillusioned. In addition, the Army received increasing criticism because it was not winning. The Army lost respect, and, consequently, it suffered from a lack of recruits. People who might have joined earlier now shunned an Army career. For the remainder of the Cold War, the Army struggled to improve its image and learn from the mistakes of Vietnam. This proved to be difficult, and the Army did not regain much of its lost respect until the 1990s.

Below: On July 29, 1993, General Colin L. Powell, Chairman of the Joint Chiefs of Staff, spoke during the groundbreaking ceremony for the Vietnam Women's Memorial in Washington, D.C.

Colin Powell

Colin Powell (1937–), an African American, began his military career when he joined the Reserve Officer Training Corps (ROTC) in college. In 1962, Powell received a one-year tour of duty in South Vietnam, where he commanded troops in combat for the first time. He returned to Vietnam for a second tour in 1968. Powell went on to serve in a number of government positions, including an appointment to the Defense Department and a job as National Security Advisor, before he became chairman of the Joint Chiefs of Staff (JCS) during the Persian Gulf War (1990–1991). When his military career ended in 1993, he was a four-star general. In 2001, he became Secretary of State for President George W. Bush's administration.

Chapter 6
The U.S. Army Evolves

Right: A young female cadet takes the oath during a ceremony at West Point.

The breakup of the Soviet Union into Russia and other independent nations in 1991 and the subsequent collapse of communism in Eastern Europe effectively ended the Cold War, and the Army has continued to evolve in various ways. Due in part to the public backlash against the Vietnam War, the Army has reshaped public perception using a media campaign and its successes during the Persian Gulf War. Not all the Army's endeavors have been successful, but its role has changed from security to peacekeeping and nation-building.

To fulfill its duties, the Army needs sufficient personnel. Following the Vietnam War, fewer people turned to the Army as a career. Consequently, the Army launched renewed public-relations campaigns, calling for people to "Be all you can be" to encourage enrollment. Recently, the Army's recruitment campaign evolved to address misconceptions about losing one's identity in a regimented Army, with advertisements illustrating an "Army of One." With the **abolition** of separate female units in 1978 and the repeal of the combat-exclusion law in 1993, women have found more career opportunities in the Army than before. Currently, women make up 14 percent of the active-duty force.

During the Clinton administration, the Army began addressing the issue of homosexuality in the military. Originally, the perception was that homosexuality was incompatible with military service. The current "don't ask, don't tell" policy requires gay, lesbian, and bisexual service people to keep their sexual orientation secret. Service people may be discharged if they admit that they are gay; are known to have had physical relations with someone of the same sex; or marry, or attempt to marry, someone of the same sex. The "don't ask, don't tell" policy is complex. The authorities have been accused of **homophobia**, and while there is a need to ensure that gay people are

U.S. Army Bases in the United States

This map shows the locations of major United States Army bases across the United States.

Washington

The Pentagon
Washington, D.C.
Fort Knox
Norfolk
Barstow
Fayetteville
Atlanta
Fort Huachuca
El Paso
Fort Jackson
Hawaii
Honolulu
San Antonio

Norman Schwarzkopf

The son of a brigadier general, Norman Schwarzkopf (below left) was educated in Europe in the early Cold War period. He graduated from West Point and earned a Master's degree in mechanical engineering at the University of Southern California, where he focused on missile engineering. Following a tour in Vietnam, he returned to West Point as an instructor. In 1969, he went back to Vietnam as a battalion commander. While there, he was wounded twice and received three Silver Stars. The culmination of Schwarzkopf's career came in 1991, as commander-in-chief of U.S. forces in Operation Desert Shield, which became Operation Desert Storm. After a six-week air campaign, U.S.-led coalition forces, commanded by General "Stormin'" Norman Schwarzkopf, achieved victory over Iraq in 100 hours.

protected from harassment, there are also concerns that homosexuality is being tolerated or even encouraged. None of this controversy has prevented the Army from fulfilling its duties.

Peacekeeping Efforts Abroad

In the post-Cold War era, the Army's focus has changed. While some troops provide security in Korea, others work with U.N. or coalition forces. In 1991, U.S. soldiers, working with coalition forces in Operation Desert Storm, ousted Iraqi forces from Kuwait. Iraqi dictator Saddam Hussein ordered the invasion of the smaller country over issues related to oil rights. Following the swift end to the conflict, the Army helped rebuild Kuwait, provided aid to the Kurds in northern Iraq, and laid the groundwork for a new peace initiative in the Middle East.

In addition to direct military action, Army units have participated in U.N. worldwide peacekeeping efforts. In 1992, following a resolution by the U.N. Security Council, the United States organized a multinational force sent into Somalia on a humanitarian **mission**, called Operation Restore Hope. Continued violence in Somalia affected the U.N. force's ability to accomplish this mission. Consequently, for a time the United States' role became more military in nature. Following a failed military mission, on which the book and movie *Black Hawk Down* are based, President Bill Clinton ordered U.S. soldiers home. Despite the failure in Somalia, the Army continued to participate in U.N. peacekeeping efforts. In 1995, U.S. Army troops deployed to the former Yugoslavia as part of a NATO force tasked with forcing Bosnian Serbs to negotiate a U.N.-backed peace treaty. Of the 36 nationalities that made up the peacekeeping force, the U.S. Army's presence was the

Left: Helping to coordinate the withdrawal of U.N. peacekeepers from Mogadishu, Somalia, Senior Airman Conrad Evans uses a computer and a satellite telephone system to transmit images to the Joint Combat Camera Center in Washington, D.C.

biggest. A brigade of troops was committed on peacekeeping exercises, backed up by a unit of Apache helicopters and various other support units.

The U.S. Army in the Twenty-first Century

Events in September 2001 pushed the Army beyond peacekeeping efforts to engage in liberation and nation-building. On September 11, 2001, terrorists flew two hijacked planes into the World Trade Center in New York City and another into the Pentagon outside of Washington D.C. A fourth hijacked plane crashed into the countryside in Pennsylvania. All aboard the planes died, and about 200 more died at the Pentagon. An estimated 2,795 people were killed when the World Trade Center towers collapsed. A government investigation linked the attacks to Afghanistan's fundamentalist Taliban government and to al-Qaeda forces based in Afghanistan. In October 2001, the Army's Rangers and Special Forces units entered Afghanistan to capture or destroy al-Qaeda forces, overthrow the Taliban, and restore Afghan government to the people. Although they have remained in Afghanistan in the months and years following September 11, 2001, occasionally meeting resistance from remnants of the Taliban, Army units have provided humanitarian aid and tried to help the Afghan people rebuild their nation. U.S. Army involvement in Afghanistan was

U.S. Army Bases Around the World

This map shows the location of major United States Army bases throughout the world.

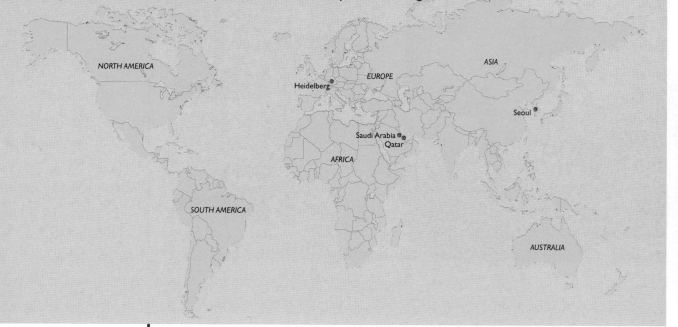

the first stage in what the government has identified as the "war on terrorism." Phase two began when the Army and coalition forces launched Operation Iraqi Freedom, an invasion of Iraq designed to overthrow dictator Saddam Hussein.

Although the actual war ended within a short period of time, armed Iraqi resistance hampered U.S. efforts to rebuild Iraq. As the U.S. presence in Iraq continued well into 2004, the growing number of U.S. casualties—both military and civilian—contributed to a feeling among many Americans that the war was destined to be far longer—and more difficult—than expected. This feeling was fed in part by other factors and events, including the suggestion that Americans may have been misled about the existence of weapons of mass destruction in Saddam's Iraq, the loss of credibility of one of the United States' strongest Iraqi allies, the videotaped beheading of a U.S. civilian, and photographic evidence of the mistreatment, abuse, or torture of a number of Iraqi prisoners at the hands of U.S. Army personnel.

The twenty-first century Army has a multitude of responsibilities and has adapted to meet the demands of a changing world. Today's Army is an

THE U.S. ARMY EVOLVES

Left: Soldiers of the 10th Mountain Division discuss an upcoming mission in Daychopan Province, Afghanistan, searching for Taliban fighters and weapons caches.

Table of Ranks

Rank	Grade	Rank	Grade
General of the Army (5-Star General)		Chief Warrant Officer	W – 2
General (4-Star General)	O – 10	Warrant Officer	W – 1
Lieutenant General (3-Star General)	O – 9	Sergeant Major of the Army	
Major General (2-Star General)	O – 8	Command Sergeant Major	E – 9
Brigadier General (1-Star General)	O – 7	Sergeant Major	E – 9
Colonel	O – 6	First Sergeant	E – 8
Lieutenant Colonel	O – 5	Master Sergeant	E – 8
Major	O – 4	Sergeant First Class	E – 7
Captain	O – 3	Staff Sergeant	E – 6
First Lieutenant	O – 2	Sergeant	E – 5
Second Lieutenant	O – 1	Corporal	E – 4
Master Warrant Officer	W – 5	Specialist	E – 4
Chief Warrant Officer	W – 4	Private First Class	E – 3
Chief Warrant Officer	W – 3	Private	E – 1/E – 2

integrated place in which people of all races and cultures are accepted and attitudes toward homosexuality are slowly changing. While it remains to be seen how the United States Army will evolve, it is clear that it will continue to not only uphold the policies and principles of the nation it serves, but also to reflect the varied social, political, and moral character of its people.

Time Line

1775:	April, British troops and U.S. colonists clash in Massachusetts; June, the Continental Army is created and George Washington is made its commander.
1776–1783:	Revolutionary War
1802:	United States Military Academy at West Point is established.
1812–1815:	War of 1812
1846–1848:	Mexican War
1861–1865:	Civil War
1898:	Spanish-American War ends in victory for the United States.
1917:	April, the United States enters World War I.
1940:	The Louisiana Maneuvers, the first large-scale war games in the United States, take place
1941:	December 7, Japanese attack Pearl Harbor.
1948:	Congress passes the Armed Forces Integration Act, setting a 2-percent strength limitation for women serving in the military.
1950:	Truman orders the Army to end all-black units by 1954; U.S. troops go to Korea; the first military advisors are sent to Korea.
1965:	U.S. participation increases in Vietnam.
1973:	Separate female units are abolished.
1991:	Operation Desert Storm.
1993:	The combat-exclusion law is repealed allowing women to serve in combat.
2001:	September 11, terrorist attacks on the World Trade Center and the Pentagon. October, Army Rangers and Special Forces begin actions in Afghanistan.
2003:	Operation Iraqi Freedom

Glossary

abolition: the act of ending the observance or effect of a practice, custom, or tradition

Allies or Allied Forces: the group of nations (including Britain, the Soviet Union, and the United States) opposing the Axis Powers in World War II

armistice: temporary suspension of hostilities by agreement between opponents in war

Axis or Axis Powers: the group of nations (initially comprising Germany and Italy, but later extended to include Japan and other countries) opposing the Allies in World War II

battle: a general military engagement with time and land limits

boycott: to refuse as a punishment or as an expression of disapproval

conscript: a person made to enroll in the military

guerrilla: a person who engages in irregular warfare especially as a member of an independent unit carrying out harassment and acts of sabotage

homophobia: irrational fear of, aversion to, or discrimination against homosexuals

infantry: foot soldiers

militia: citizens attending part-time military training and called up when needed

mission: a task with which a person or a group is charged

munitions: military weapons: ammunition or equipment

regular army: professional members of the armed forces

secede: to withdraw from an organization

segregate: to separate or set apart from others or the general population, especially according to race

Further Information

Books:

Anderson, Christopher J. *The U.S. Army Today: From the End of the Cold War to the Present Day.* Philadelphia: Chelsea House Publishers, 1999.

Bartlett, Richard and Ellen Hopkins. *United States Army.* Chicago: Heinemann Library, 2003.

Goldberg, Jan. *Green Berets: The U.S. Army Special Forces.* New York: Rosen Publishing Group, 2003.

Green, Michael, Gladys Green, and Steve Maguire. *The U.S. Army Rangers at War.* Mankato, MN: Capstone Press, 2003.

Sawyer, Susan. *The Army in Action.* Berkeley Heights, NJ: Enslow Publishers, Inc., 2001.

Web sites:

Go Army

www.goarmy.com/army101/

Learn about the Army, and how a person can serve or become a soldier.

America's Army

www.americasarmy.com/

The Army from a soldier's point of view, an online simulation game.

United States Military Academy at West Point

www.usma.edu/

Information about West Point, including mission, admissions, and academic programs.

United States Army War College

carlisle-www.army.mil/

In addition to training officers, the Army War College has research facilities.

The United States Army

www.army.mil/

This Web site has links to other sites with information about recruiting, the ROTC, the National Guard, and Army Reserve, as well as current operations.